TABLE OF CONTENTS

INTRODUCTION 2

CAKE MIX RECIPE #1
Gingerbread Quilt. 4
Sherbet Quilt 8

CAKE MIX RECIPE #2
Fondant Quilt 12
Taffy Quilt. 16

CAKE MIX RECIPE #3
Creme Brulee Quilt 20
Sundae Quilt 22

CAKE MIX RECIPE #4
Marzipan Quilt 30
Parfait Quilt 34

CAKE MIX RECIPE #5
Banana Split Quilt 38
Ganache Quilt 42

CAKE MIX RECIPE #6
Fruitcake Quilt 46
Meringue Quilt 50

CAKE MIX RECIPE #7
Buttercream Quilt. 54
Tiramisu Quilt. 58

CAKE MIX RECIPE #8
Cheesecake Quilt 62
Petit Four Quilt 66

INTRODUCTION

Welcome to the scrumptious world of Cake Mixes! Grab ahold of the nearest Layer Cake and hang on because this is bound to be a wild ride!

After sampling the delicious Cake Mix Recipe Cards by Miss Rosie's Quilt Co., It's Sew Emma has cooked up some flavorful combinations in our quilty test kitchen and we are excited to have you try them! But first, let's go over the basics.

WHAT IN THE WAFFLE ARE LAYER CAKES AND CAKE MIXES?

Good question! Layer Cakes are precuts created by Moda Fabrics that include 42 - 10" fabric squares. They are offered in print collections and Bella Solids. We love to pair them with the Cake Mixes.

Cake Mixes are pads of triangle paper designed to be used with Moda Layer Cakes. They contain 44 to 45 Recipe Cards of pre-printed paper that create different types of units used to build quilt blocks. Inside you will also find "Basic Baking Techniques" with simple instructions and suggestions as well as several finished block ideas. At the moment there are eight different Cake Mixes available, and in this book we have two quilts for each pad for a total of 16 quilts.

We simply love the Cake Mixes as triangle paper. You will have less waste than creating these units with traditional methods and your units will be more accurate!

CAKE MIX #1
4 - 4" HALF SQUARE TRIANGLES
1 - 8" HALF SQUARE TRIANGLE

CAKE MIX #2
10 - 2 ¼" HALF SQUARE TRIANGLES
2 - 4 ½" HALF SQUARE TRIANGLES

CAKE MIX #3
18 - 2" HALF SQUARE TRIANGLES

CAKE MIX #4
8 - 3 ¾" HALF SQUARE TRIANGLES
OR
8 - 4" HALF SQUARE TRIANGLES

HOW IN THE CINNAMON ROLLS DO I USE THESE?

Following the "Basic Baking Techniques" inside the Cake Mixes . . .

#1 Layer two Layer Cake squares right sides together, with a Cake Mix Recipe Card on top.

#2 Pin the stack together in a few places to keep it from shifting, being careful to avoid the dotted sewing lines.

#3 Shorten your stitch length to 1.5 and begin sewing the stack together where the sheet is marked ★Start.

#4 Follow the arrows and numbers and stitch along the dotted lines.

#5 Cut along the solid lines starting with the outside edges.

#6 Tear off the paper.

#7 Press and clip off dog ears.

Now that you have all your units prepared, it's time to get baking. Select a mouthwatering pattern from the following pages and bake – I mean quilt!

CAKE MIX #5
4 - 3 ½" HALF SQUARE TRIANGLES
4 - 3 ½" FOUR PATCH UNITS

CAKE MIX #6
8 - 2" HALF SQUARE TRIANGLES
8 - 2" RAIL FENCE UNITS
2 - 2" SQUARES

CAKE MIX #7
4 - 3" HALF SQUARE TRIANGLES
16 - 1 ½" HALF SQUARE TRIANGLES

CAKE MIX #8
4 - 3" HALF SQUARE TRIANGLES
30 - 1" HALF SQUARE TRIANGLES

GINGERBREAD QUILT

68 ½" x 92 ½"

QUILT INGREDIENTS

One	Cake Mix Recipe #1	
	35 - Recipe Cards	Blocks
One	Print Layer Cake	
	35 - 10" squares	Blocks
One	Solid Layer Cake	
	35 - 10" squares	Blocks
2 yards	Solid	
	35 - 4 ½" squares	Blocks
	9 - 4 ½" x WOF strips	Border
⅞ yard	Binding	
	9 - 2 ½" x WOF strips	
5 ¾ yards	Backing	

LET'S GET STARTED

With right sides facing, layer a Print 10" square with a Solid 10" square.

Follow instructions on page 3.

Large Half Square Triangle Unit should measure 8 ½" x 8 ½".

Small Half Square Triangle Unit should measure 4 ½" x 4 ½".

Make 1 Large Half Square Triangle Unit from each Recipe Card.

Make 35 total.

Make 4 Small Half Square Triangle Units from each Recipe Card.

Make 140 total.

Assemble Unit using matching fabric.

Top Gingerbread Unit should measure 4 ½" x 8 ½".

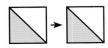

Make 1 Unit from each Recipe Card.

Make 35 total.

Assemble Unit using matching fabric.

Left Gingerbread Unit should measure 4 ½" x 8 ½".

Make 1 Unit from each Recipe Card.

Make 35 total.

Assemble Block using matching fabric and one Solid 4 ½" square.

Gingerbread Block should measure 12 ½" x 12 ½".

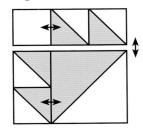 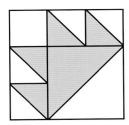

Make 1 Block from each Recipe Card.

Make 35 total.

GINGERBREAD QUILT

FINISH IT UP

Assemble Quilt Center. Press rows in alternating directions.

Quilt Center should measure 60 ½" x 84 ½".

Piece the Solid 4 ½" x WOF strips end to end.

Subcut into:

      2 - 4 ½" x 84 ½" strips (Side Borders)

      2 - 4 ½" x 68 ½" strips (Top and Bottom Borders)

Attach the Side Borders.

Attach the Top and Bottom Borders.

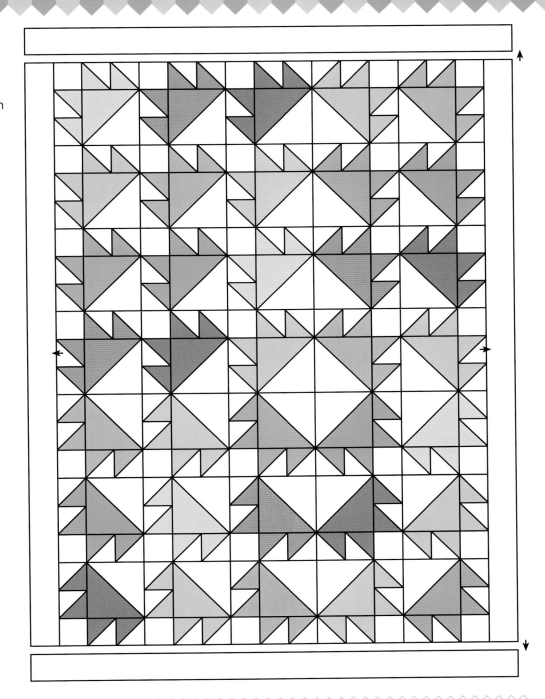

Piece the 2 ½" x WOF strips end to end for binding.

Quilt and bind as desired.

SHERBET QUILT

QUILT INGREDIENTS

One	Cake Mix Recipe #1	
	36 - Recipe Cards	Blocks
One	Print Layer Cake	
	36 - 10" squares	Blocks
One	Solid Layer Cake	
	36 - 10" squares	Blocks
4 ¼ yards	Solid	
	36 - 4 ½" squares	Blocks
	6 - 4 ½" x 24 ½" strips	Sashing
	5 - 4 ½" x WOF strips	Sashing
	11 - 6 ½" x WOF strips	Border
⅞ yard	Binding	
	10 - 2 ½" x WOF strips	
8 ⅝ yards	Backing	

LET'S GET STARTED

With right sides facing, layer a Print 10" square with a Solid 10" square.

Follow instructions on page 3.

Large Half Square Triangle Unit should measure 8 ½" x 8 ½".

Small Half Square Triangle Unit should measure 4 ½" x 4 ½".

Make 1 Large Half Square Triangle Unit from each Recipe Card.

Make 36 total.

Make 4 Small Half Square Triangle Units from each Recipe Card.

Make 144 total.

Assemble Unit using matching fabric.

Top Sherbet Unit should measure 4 ½" x 8 ½".

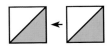

Make 1 Unit from each Recipe Card.

Make 36 total.

Assemble Unit using matching fabric.

Left Sherbet Unit should measure 4 ½" x 8 ½".

Make 1 Unit from each Recipe Card.

Make 36 total.

Assemble Unit using matching fabric and one Solid 4 ½" square.

Sherbet Unit should measure 12 ½" x 12 ½".

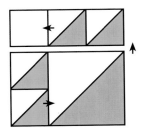 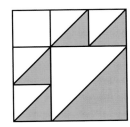

Make 1 Unit from each Recipe Card.

Make 36 total.

Assemble Block.

Sherbet Block should measure 24 ½" x 24 ½".

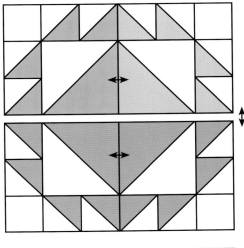

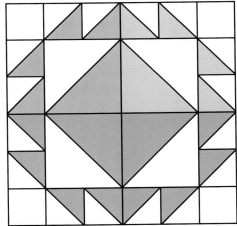

Make 9 total.

SHERBET QUILT

FINISH IT UP

Piece the Solid 4 ½" x WOF strips end to end.

Subcut into:

  2 - 4 ½" x 80 ½" strips (Sashing)

Assemble Quilt Center using the Sashing. Press toward the Solid.

Quilt Center should measure 80 ½" x 80 ½".

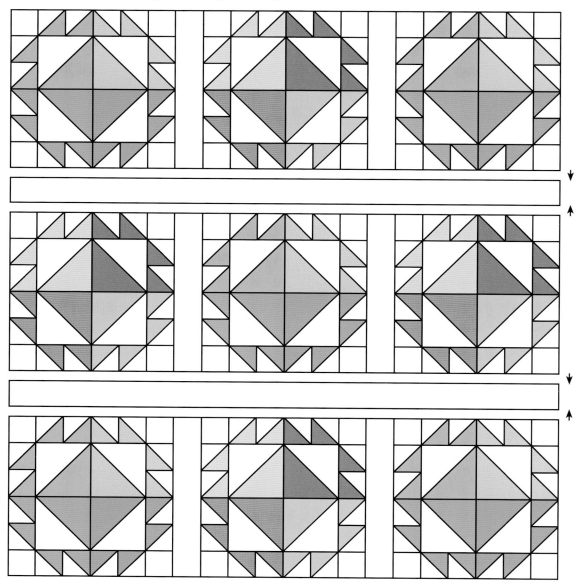

Piece the Solid 6 ½" x WOF strips end to end.

Subcut into:

      2 - 6 ½" x 80 ½" strips (Side Borders)

      2 - 6 ½" x 92 ½" strips (Top and Bottom Borders)

Attach the Side Borders.

Attach the Top and Bottom Borders.

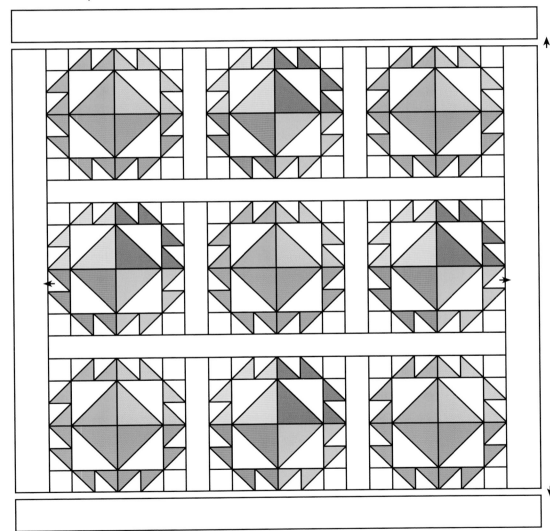

Piece the 2 ½" x WOF strips end to end for binding.

Quilt and bind as desired.

FONDANT QUILT

QUILT INGREDIENTS

One	Cake Mix Recipe #2	
	32 - Recipe Cards	Blocks
One	Print Layer Cake	
	32 - 10" squares	Blocks
One	Solid Layer Cake	
	32 - 10" squares	Blocks
2 ¼ yards	Solid	
	12 - 2 ¾" x 14" rectangles	Sashing
	6 - 2 ¾" x WOF strips	Sashing
	8 - 5" x WOF strips	Border
¾ yard	Binding	
	8 - 2 ½" x WOF strips	
4 ½ yards	Backing	

LET'S GET STARTED

With right sides facing, layer a Print 10" square with a Solid 10" square.

Follow instructions on page 3.

Large Half Square Triangle Unit should measure 5" x 5".

Small Half Square Triangle Unit should measure 2 ¾" x 2 ¾".

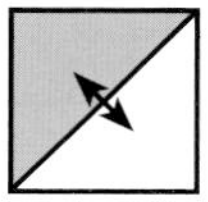

Make 2 Large Half Square Triangle Units from each Recipe Card.

Make 64 total.

Make 10 Small Half Square Triangle Units from each Recipe Card.

Make 320 total.

Each Fondant Block uses two coordinating
Print 10" squares (Pair).

Assemble Unit using coordinating fabric.

Outside Fondant Unit should measure 5" x 5".

Make 4 Units from each Pair.

Make 64 total.

Assemble Unit using coordinating fabric.

Center Fondant Unit should measure 5" x 5".

Make 1 Unit from each Pair.

Make 16 total.

Assemble Block using coordinating fabric.

Fondant Block should measure 14" x 14".

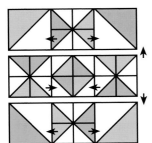 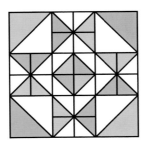

Make 1 Block from each Pair.

Make 16 total.

FONDANT QUILT

FINISH IT UP

Piece the Solid 2 ¾" x WOF strips end to end.

Subcut into:

      3 - 2 ¾" x 61 ¼" strips (Sashing)

Assemble Quilt Center using the Sashing. Press toward the Solid.

Quilt Center should measure 61 ¼" x 61 ¼".

Piece the Solid 5" x WOF strips end to end.

Subcut into:

      2 - 5" x 61 ¼" strips (Side Borders)

      2 - 5" x 70 ¼" strips (Top and Bottom Borders)

Attach the Side Borders.

Attach the Top and Bottom Borders.

Piece the 2 ½" x WOF strips end to end for binding.

Quilt and bind as desired.

TAFFY QUILT

65 ¾" x 65 ¾"

QUILT INGREDIENTS

One	Cake Mix Recipe #2	
	32 - Recipe Cards	Blocks
One	Print Layer Cake	
	32 - 10" squares	Blocks
One	Solid Layer Cake	
	32 - 10" squares	Blocks
1 ⅝ yards	Solid	
	12 - 2 ¾" x 14" rectangles	Sashing
	12 - 2 ¾" x WOF strips	Sashing & Border
¾ yard	Binding	
	8 - 2 ½" x WOF strips	
4 ¼ yards	Backing	

LET'S GET STARTED

With right sides facing, layer a Print 10" square with a Solid 10" square.

Follow instructions on page 3.

Large Half Square Triangle Unit should measure 5" x 5".

Small Half Square Triangle Unit should measure 2 ¾" x 2 ¾".

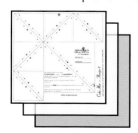

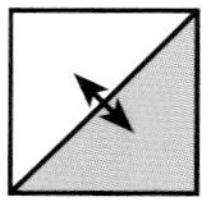

Make 2 Large Half Square Triangle Units from each Recipe Card.

Make 64 total.

Make 10 Small Half Square Triangle Units from each Recipe Card.

Make 320 total.

Each Taffy Block uses two coordinating Print 10" squares (Pair).

Assemble Unit using matching fabric.

Top Taffy Unit should measure 2 ¾" x 5".

Make 2 Units from each Recipe Card.

Make 64 total.

Assemble Unit using matching fabric.

Left Taffy Unit should measure 2 ¾" x 5".

Make 2 Units from each Recipe Card.

Make 64 total.

Assemble Unit using coordinating fabric. Pay close attention to unit placement.

Taffy Unit One should measure 7 ¼" x 7 ¼".

Make 2 Units from each Pair.

Make 32 total.

Assemble Unit using coordinating fabric. Pay close attention to unit placement.

Taffy Unit Two should measure 7 ¼" x 7 ¼".

Make 2 Units from each Pair.

Make 32 total.

Assemble Block using coordinating fabric.

Taffy Block should measure 14" x 14".

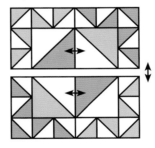 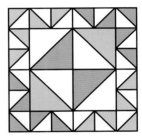

Make 1 Block from each Pair.

Make 16 total.

TAFFY QUILT

FINISH IT UP

Piece the Solid 2 ¾″ x WOF strips end to end.

Subcut into:

> 5 - 2 ¾″ x 61 ¼″ strips (Sashing and Side Borders)
>
> 2 - 2 ¾″ x 65 ¾″ strips (Top and Bottom Borders)

Assemble Quilt Center using the Sashing. Pay close attention to block placement. Press toward the Solid.

Quilt Center should measure 61 ¼″ x 61 ¼″.

Attach the Side Borders.

Attach the Top and Bottom Borders.

Piece the 2 ½" x WOF strips end to end for binding.

Quilt and bind as desired.

CREME BRULEE QUILT

QUILT INGREDIENTS

One	Cake Mix Recipe #3	
	36 - Recipe Cards	Blocks
One	Print Layer Cake	
	36 - 10" squares	Blocks
One	Solid Layer Cake	
	36 - 10" squares	Blocks
1 ⅝ yards	Solid	
	84 - 2 ½" x 8 ½" rectangles	Sashing
⅝ yard	Binding	
	7 - 2 ½" x WOF strips	
4 ⅛ yards	Backing	

LET'S GET STARTED

With right sides facing, layer a Print 10" square with a Solid 10" square.

Follow instructions on page 3.

Half Square Triangle Unit should measure 2 ½" x 2 ½".

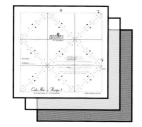

Make 18 Half Square Triangle Units from each Recipe Card.

Make 648 total.

Assemble Block using matching fabric.

Creme Brulee Block should measure 8 ½" x 8 ½".

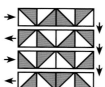

Make 1 Block from each Recipe Card.

Make 36 total.

FINISH IT UP

Assemble Quilt Center using the Sashing. Pay close attention to block placement. Press toward the Solid.

Quilt Center should measure 62 ½" x 62 ½".

YOU WILL NOT USE ALL
HALF SQUARE TRIANGLE UNITS!

Piece the 2 ½" x WOF strips end to end for binding.

Quilt and bind as desired.

SUNDAE QUILT

90 ½" x 90 ½"

QUILT INGREDIENTS

One	Cake Mix Recipe #3	
	30 - Recipe Cards	Blocks
One	Print Layer Cake	
	36 - 10" squares	Blocks
One	Solid Layer Cake	
	30 - 10" squares	Blocks
6 ⅝ yards	Solid	
	84 - 2 ½" x 10 ½" rectangles	Sashing
	72 - 2 ½" x 4 ½" rectangles	Blocks
	36 - 2 ½" squares	Blocks
	72 - 1 ½" x 10 ½" rectangles	Blocks
	72 - 1 ½" x 8 ½" rectangles	Blocks
	36 - 1 ½" x 3 ½" rectangles	Blocks
	36 - 1 ½" x 2 ½" rectangles	Blocks
	9 - 2 ½" x WOF strips	Border
	10 - 4 ½" x WOF strips	Border
⅞ yard	Binding	
	10 - 2 ½" x WOF strips	
8 ⅜ yards	Backing	

LET'S GET STARTED

Divide the Print Layer Cake into two groups:

- Group A has six 10" squares
- Group B has thirty 10" squares

Cut each Group A Print 10" square into:

- 6 - 1 ½" x 4 ½" rectangles
- 6 - 1 ½" x 3 ½" rectangles

These will be used for the basket handles.

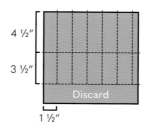

With right sides facing, layer a Group B Print 10" square with a Solid 10" square.

Follow instructions on page 3.

Half Square Triangle Unit should measure 2 ½" x 2 ½".

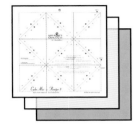

Make 18 Half Square Triangle Units from 30 Recipe Cards.

Make 540 total.

Each Sundae Block uses a coordinating Group A Print 10" square and a Group B Print 10" square (Pair).

Assemble Unit using matching fabric and one Solid 2 ½" x 4 ½" rectangle.

Top Left Sundae Unit should measure 4 ½" x 4 ½".

Make 36 total.

Assemble Unit using matching fabric and one Solid 2 ½" square.

Bottom Left Sundae Unit should measure 4 ½" x 4 ½".

Make 36 total.

Assemble Unit using matching fabric and one Solid 2 ½" x 4 ½" rectangle.

Bottom Right Sundae Unit should measure 4 ½" x 4 ½".

Make 36 total.

Assemble Unit using one Solid 1 ½" x 2 ½" rectangle and one Solid 1 ½" x 3 ½" rectangle.

Partial Top Right Sundae Unit should measure 3 ½" x 3 ½".

Make 36 total.

Assemble Unit using one coordinating Print 1 ½" x 3 ½" rectangle and one matching Print 1 ½" x 4 ½" rectangle.

Top Right Sundae Unit should measure 4 ½" x 4 ½".

Make 36 total.

SUNDAE QUILT

Assemble Unit using matching fabric.

Sundae Unit should measure 8 ½″ x 8 ½″.

Make 36 total.

Assemble Block using two Solid 1 ½″ x 8 ½″ rectangles and two Solid 1 ½″ x 10 ½″ rectangles.

Sundae Block should measure 10 ½″ x 10 ½″.

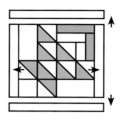 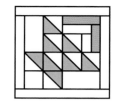

Make 36 total.

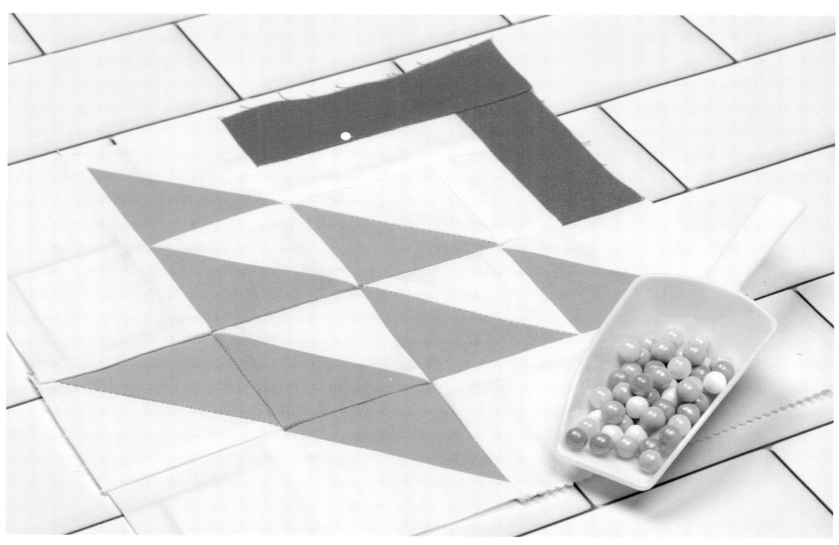

FINISH IT UP

Assemble Quilt Center using the Sashing. Press toward the Solid.

Quilt Center should measure 74 ½" x 74 ½".

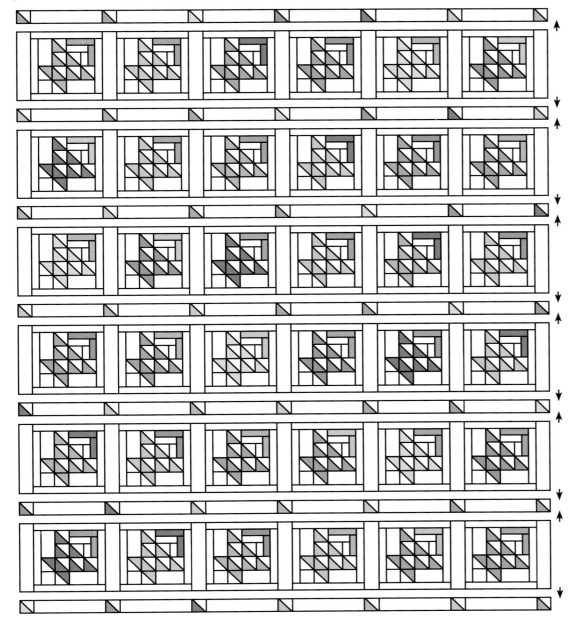

SUNDAE QUILT

Piece the Solid 2 ½" x WOF strips end to end.

Subcut into:

      2 - 2 ½" x 74 ½" strips (Side Inner Borders)

      2 - 2 ½" x 78 ½" strips (Top and Bottom Inner Borders)

Attach the Side Inner Borders.

Attach the Top and Bottom Inner Borders.

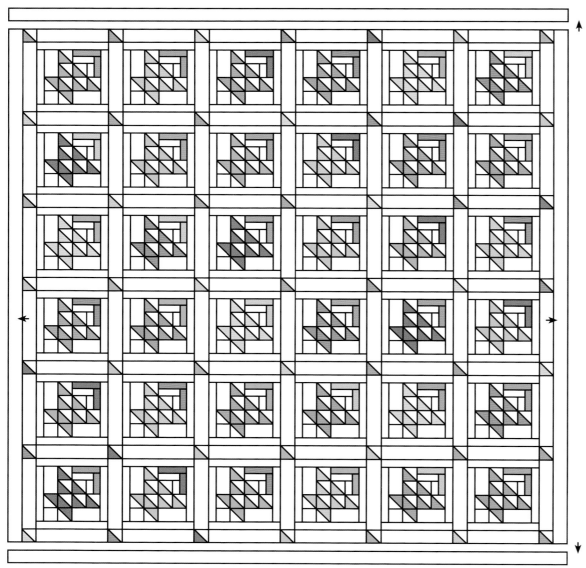

Assemble Border using 39 Half Square Triangle Units.

Side Middle Border should measure 2 ½" x 78 ½".

Make 2.

Assemble Border using 41 Half Square Triangle Units.

Top and Bottom Middle Border should measure 2 ½" x 82 ½".

Make 2.

YOU WILL NOT USE ALL
HALF SQUARE TRIANGLE UNITS!

SUNDAE QUILT

Attach the Side Middle Borders.

Attach the Top and Bottom Middle Borders.

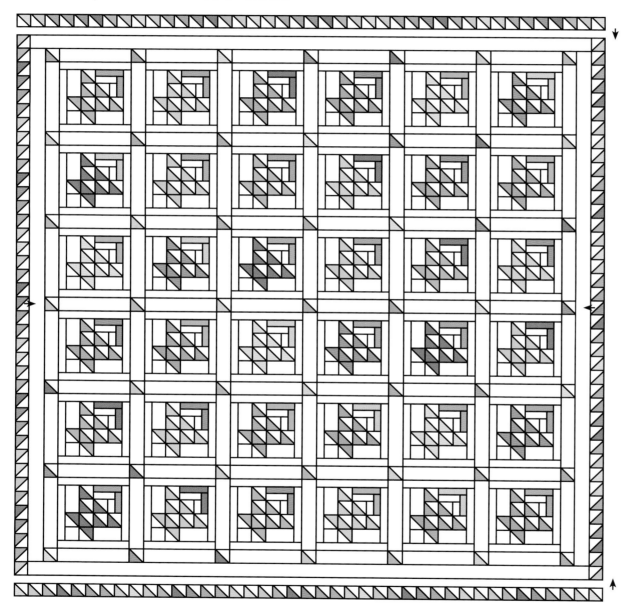

Piece the Solid 4 ½" x WOF strips end to end.

Subcut into:

  2 - 4 ½" x 82 ½" strips (Side Outer Borders)

  2 - 4 ½" x 90 ½" strips (Top and Bottom Outer Borders)

Attach the Side Outer Borders.

Attach the Top and Bottom Outer Borders.

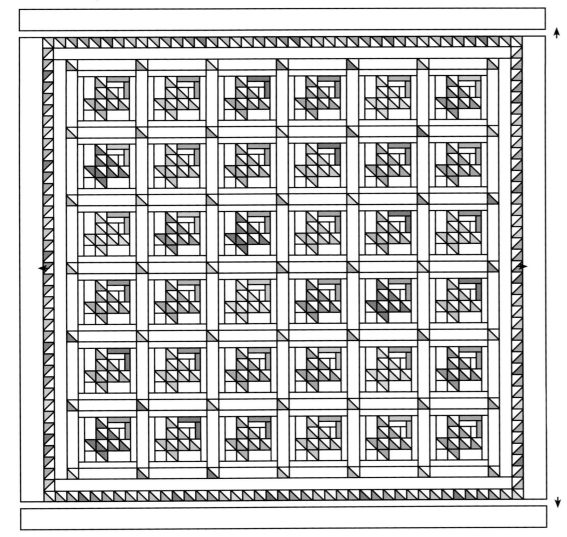

Piece the 2 ½" x WOF strips end to end for binding.

Quilt and bind as desired.

MARZIPAN QUILT

QUILT INGREDIENTS

One	Cake Mix Recipe #4	
	32 - Recipe Cards	Blocks
One	Print Layer Cake	
	32 - 10" squares	Blocks
One	Solid Layer Cake	
	32 - 10" squares	Blocks
4 ⅝ yards	Solid	
	12 - 4 ½" x 16 ½" rectangles	Sashing
	7 - 4 ½" x WOF strips	Sashing
	11 - 8 ½" x WOF strips	Border
⅞ yard	Binding	
	10 - 2 ½" x WOF strips	
8 ⅝ yards	Backing	

LET'S GET STARTED

With right sides facing, layer a Print 10" square with a Solid 10" square.

Follow instructions on page 3.

Cut on the 4" cutting line.

Half Square Triangle Unit should measure 4 ½" x 4 ½".

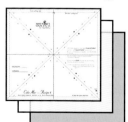

Make 8 Half Square Triangle Units from each Recipe Card.

Make 256 total.

Each Marzipan Block uses two coordinating Print 10" squares (Pair).

Assemble Block using coordinating fabric.

Marzipan Block should measure 16 ½" x 16 ½".

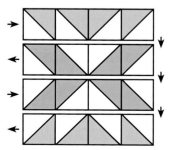 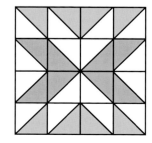

Make 1 Block from each Pair.

Make 16 total.

FINISH IT UP

Piece the Solid 4 ½" x WOF strips end to end.

Subcut into:

      3 - 4 ½" x 76 ½" strips (Sashing)

Assemble Quilt Center using the Sashing. Pay close attention to block placement. Press toward the Solid.

Quilt Center should measure 76 ½" x 76 ½".

MARZIPAN QUILT

Piece the Solid 8 ½" x WOF strips end to end.

Subcut into:

2 - 8 ½" x 76 ½" strips (Side Borders)

2 - 8 ½" x 92 ½" strips (Top and Bottom Borders)

Attach the Side Borders.

Attach the Top and Bottom Borders.

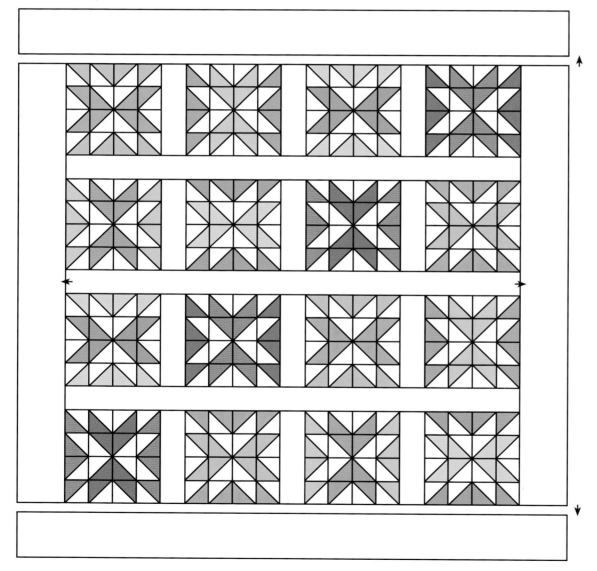

Piece the 2 ½" x WOF strips end to end for binding.

Quilt and bind as desired.

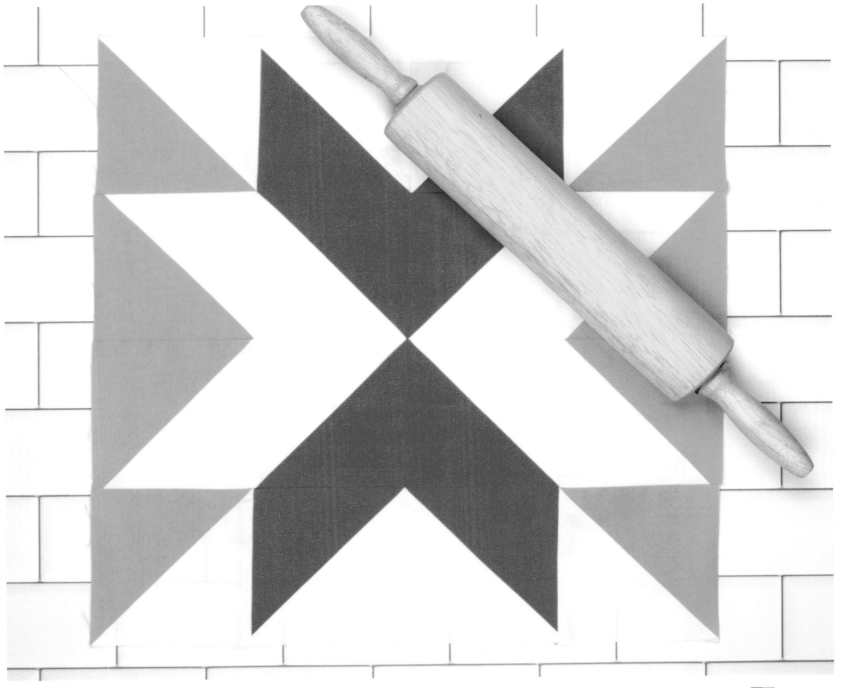

QUILT INGREDIENTS

One	Cake Mix Recipe #4	
	33 - Recipe Cards	Blocks
One	Print Layer Cake	
	33 - 10" squares	Blocks
One	Solid Layer Cake	
	33 - 10" squares	Blocks
2 yards	Solid	
	16 - 4 ½" squares	Sashing
	80 - 1 ½" x 8 ½" rectangles	Sashing
	7 - 2 ½" x WOF strips	Border
⅝ yard	Binding	
	7 - 2 ½" x WOF strips	
4 yards	Backing	

LET'S GET STARTED

Divide the Print Layer Cake into two groups:

- Group A has thirteen 10" squares
- Group B has twenty 10" squares

With right sides facing, layer a Group A Print 10" square with a Solid 10" square.

Follow instructions on page 3.

Cut on the 4" cutting line.

Large Half Square Triangle Unit should measure 4 ½" x 4 ½".

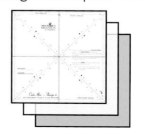

Make 8 Large Half Square Triangle Units from 13 Recipe Cards.

Make 104 total.

Assemble Block using matching fabric.

Parfait Block should measure 8 ½" x 8 ½".

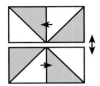

Make 2 Blocks from 13 Recipe Cards.

Make 26 total. You will not use 1 Block.

With right sides facing, layer a Group B Print 10" square with a Solid 10" square.

Follow instructions on page 3.

Cut on the 3 ¾" cutting line.

Small Half Square Triangle Unit should measure 4 ¼" x 4 ¼".

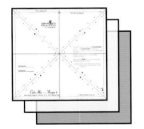

Make 8 Small Half Square Triangle Units from 20 Recipe Cards.

Make 160 total.

With right sides facing, layer two matching Small Half Square Triangle Units making sure seams are in the same direction.

Draw a diagonal line on the wrong side of the top Small Half Square Triangle Unit in the opposite direction of the seams.

Stitch ¼" from each side of the drawn line.

Trim Hourglass Unit to measure 2 ½" x 2 ½".

Make 8 Hourglass Units from 20 Recipe Cards.

Make 160 total.

Assemble Unit using matching fabric.

Partial Sashing Unit should measure 2 ½" x 8 ½".

Make 2 Units from 20 Recipe Cards.

Make 40 total.

Assemble Block using two Solid 1 ½" x 8 ½" rectangles.

Sashing Block should measure 4 ½" x 8 ½".

Make 2 Blocks from 20 Recipe Cards.

Make 40 total.

PARFAIT QUILT

FINISH IT UP

Assemble Quilt Center using the Sashing. Press toward the Parfait Blocks and the Solid.
Quilt Center should measure 56 ½" x 56 ½".

Piece the Solid 2 ½" x WOF strips end to end.

Subcut into:

  2 - 2 ½" x 56 ½" strips (Side Borders)

  2 - 2 ½" x 60 ½" strips (Top and Bottom Borders)

Attach the Side Borders.

Attach the Top and Bottom Borders.

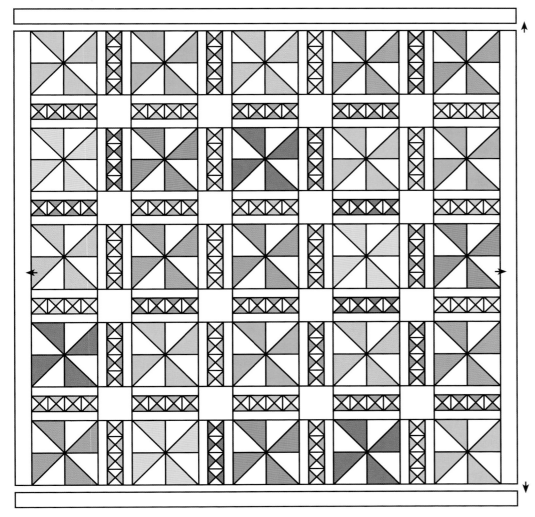

Piece the 2 ½" x WOF strips end to end for binding.

Quilt and bind as desired.

BANANA SPLIT QUILT

QUILT INGREDIENTS

One	Cake Mix Recipe #5	
	36 - Recipe Cards	Blocks
One	Print Layer Cake	
	36 - 10" squares	Blocks
One	Solid Layer Cake	
	36 - 10" squares	Blocks
4 ¾ yards	Solid	
	72 - 4" squares	Blocks
	60 - 4" x 11" rectangles	Sashing
	11 - 5 ¾" x WOF strips	Border
⅞ yard	Binding	
	10 - 2 ½" x WOF strips	
8 ½ yards	Backing	

LET'S GET STARTED

With right sides facing, layer a Print 10" square with a Solid 10" square.

Follow instructions on page 3.

Half Square Triangle Unit should measure 4" x 4".

Two Patch Unit should measure 2 ¼" x 4".

Make 4 Half Square Triangle Units from each Recipe Card.
Make 144 total.

Make 8 Two Patch Units from each Recipe Card.
Make 288 total.

Assemble Unit using matching fabric.

Four Patch Unit should measure 4" x 4".

Make 4 Units from each Recipe Card.

Make 144 total.

Assemble Unit using matching fabric and one Solid 4" square.

Outside Banana Split Unit should measure 4" x 11".

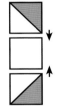 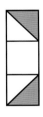

Make 2 Units from each Recipe Card.

Make 72 total.

Assemble Unit using matching fabric.

Inside Banana Split Unit should measure 4" x 11".

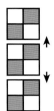 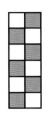

Make 1 Unit from each Recipe Card.

Make 36 total.

Assemble Block using matching fabric.

Banana Split Block should measure 11" x 11".

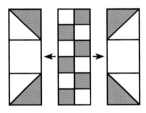 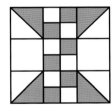

Make 1 Block from each Recipe Card.

Make 36 total.

BANANA SPLIT QUILT

FINISH IT UP

Assemble Quilt Center using the Sashing. Pay close attention to block placement. Press toward the Solid.

Quilt Center should measure 81" x 81".

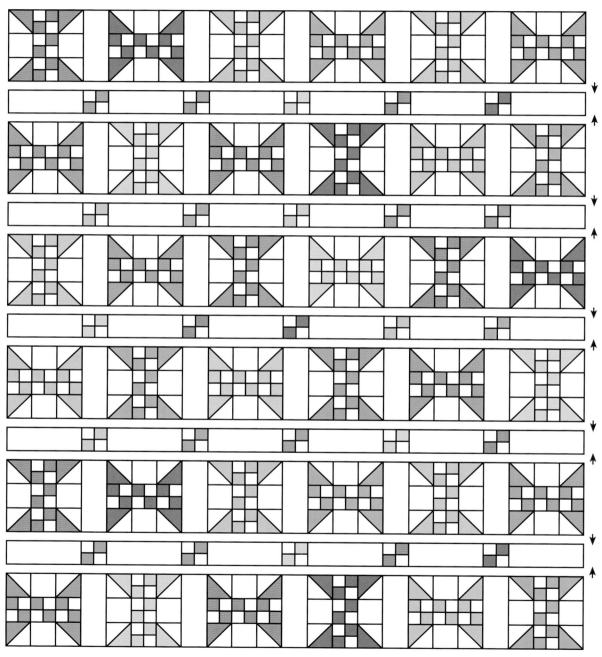

YOU WILL NOT USE ALL FOUR PATCH UNITS!

Piece the Solid 5 ¾" x WOF strips end to end.

Subcut into:

  2 - 5 ¾" x 81" strips (Side Borders)

  2 - 5 ¾" x 91 ½" strips (Top and Bottom Borders)

Attach the Side Borders.

Attach the Top and Bottom Borders.

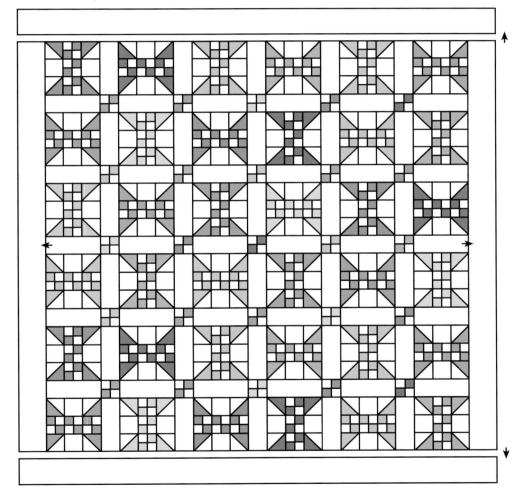

Piece the 2 ½" x WOF strips end to end for binding.

Quilt and bind as desired.

GANACHE QUILT

75 ¾″ x 75 ¾″

QUILT INGREDIENTS

One	Cake Mix Recipe #5	
	32 - Recipe Cards	Blocks
One	Print Moda Layer Cake	
	32 - 10″ squares	Blocks
One	Solid Layer Cake	
	32 - 10″ squares	Blocks
2 ⅞ yards	Solid	
	56 - 2 ¼″ x 7 ½″ rectangles	Sashing
	13 - 2 ¼″ x WOF strips	Sashing
	9 - 4″ x WOF strips	Border
⅞ yard	Binding	
	9 - 2 ½″ x WOF strips	
7 ¼ yards	Backing	

LET'S GET STARTED

With right sides facing, layer a Print 10″ square with a Solid 10″ square.

Follow instructions on page 3.

Half Square Triangle Unit should measure 4″ x 4″.

Two Patch Unit should measure 2 ¼″ x 4″.

Make 4 Half Square Triangle Units from each Recipe Card.

Make 128 total.

Make 8 Two Patch Units from each Recipe Card.

Make 256 total.

Each Ganache Block uses two coordinating Print 10″ squares (Pair).

Assemble Unit using matching fabric.

Four Patch Unit should measure 4″ x 4″.

Make 4 Units from each Recipe Card.

Make 128 total.

Assemble Block using coordinating fabric.

Ganache Block should measure 7 ½″ x 7 ½″.

Make 64 total.

GANACHE QUILT

FINISH IT UP

Piece the Solid 2 ¼" x WOF strips end to end.

Subcut into:

      7 - 2 ¼" x 68 ¾" strips (Sashing)

Assemble Quilt Center using the Sashing. Pay close attention to block placement. Press toward the Solid.

Quilt Center should measure 68 ¾" x 68 ¾".

Piece the Solid 4" x WOF strips end to end.

Subcut into:

      2 - 4" x 68 ¾" strips (Side Borders)

      2 - 4" x 75 ¾" strips (Top and Bottom Borders)

Attach the Side Borders.

Attach the Top and Bottom Borders.

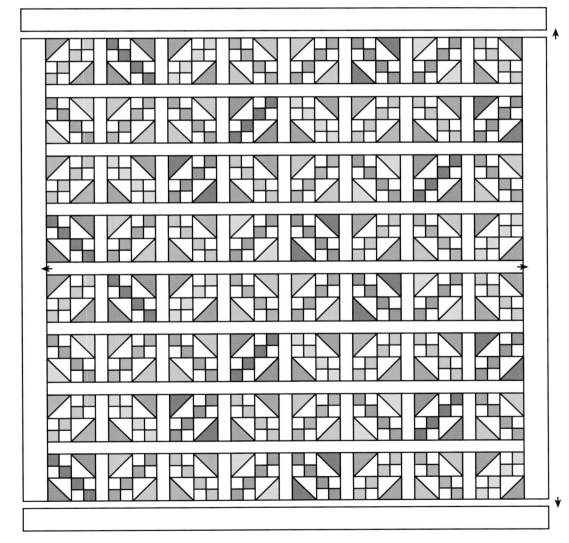

Piece the 2 ½" x WOF strips end to end for binding.

Quilt and bind as desired.

FRUITCAKE QUILT

QUILT INGREDIENTS

One	Cake Mix Recipe #6	
	35 - Recipe Cards	Blocks
One	Print Layer Cake	
	35 - 10" squares	Blocks
One	Solid Layer Cake	
	35 - 10" squares	Blocks
3 ⅛ yards	Solid	
	60 - 2 ½" x 6 ½" rectangles	Sashing
	14 - 2 ½" x WOF strips	Sashing
	9 - 4 ½" x WOF strips	Border
⅞ yard	Binding	
	9 - 2 ½" x WOF strips	
5 ⅜ yards	Backing	

LET'S GET STARTED

With right sides facing, layer a Print 10" square with a Solid 10" square.

Follow instructions on page 3.

Half Square Triangle Unit should measure 2 ½" x 2 ½".

Rail Fence Unit should measure 2 ½" x 2 ½".

Square Unit should measure 2 ½" x 2 ½".

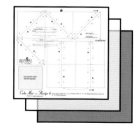

Make 8 Half Square Triangle Units from each Recipe Card.

Make 280 total.

Make 8 Rail Fence Units from each Recipe Card.

Make 280 total.

Make 2 Square Units from each Recipe Card.

Make 70 total.

Assemble Block using matching fabric.

Fruitcake Block One should measure 6 ½″ x 6 ½″.

Make 1 Block from each Recipe Card.

Make 35 total.

Assemble Block using matching fabric.

Fruitcake Block Two should measure 6 ½″ x 6 ½″.

Make 1 Block from each Recipe Card.

Make 35 total.

FRUITCAKE QUILT

FINISH IT UP

Piece the Solid 2 ½" x WOF strips end to end.

Subcut into:

> 9 - 2 ½" x 54 ½" strips (Sashing)

Assemble Quilt Center using the Sashing. Pay close attention to block placement. Press toward the Solid.

Quilt Center should measure 54 ½" x 78 ½".

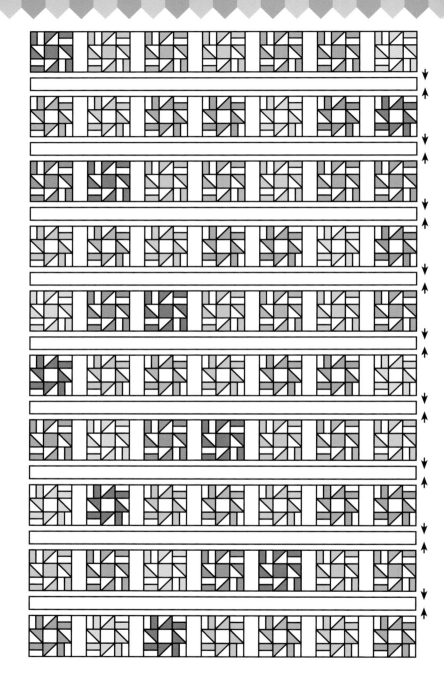

Piece the Solid 4 ½" x WOF strips end to end.

Subcut into:

      2 - 4 ½" x 78 ½" strips (Side Borders)

      2 - 4 ½" x 62 ½" strips (Top and Bottom Borders)

Attach the Side Borders.

Attach the Top and Bottom Borders.

Piece the 2 ½" x WOF strips end to end for binding.

Quilt and bind as desired.

MERINGUE QUILT

50 ½" x 68 ½"

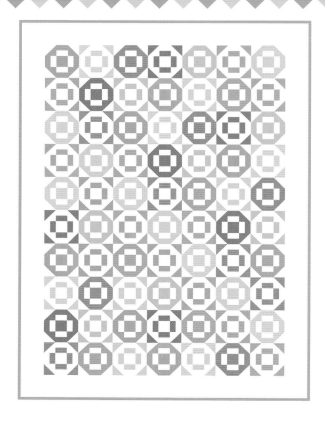

QUILT INGREDIENTS

One	Cake Mix Recipe #6	
	35 - Recipe Cards	Blocks
One	Print Layer Cake	
	35 - 10" squares	Blocks
One	Solid Layer Cake	
	35 - 10" squares	Blocks
1 ⅛ yards	Solid	
	7 - 4 ½" x WOF strips	Border
⅝ yard	Binding	
	7 - 2 ½" x WOF strips	
3 ⅜ yards	Backing	

LET'S GET STARTED

With right sides facing, layer a Print 10" square with a Solid 10" square.

Follow instructions on page 3.

Half Square Triangle Unit should measure 2 ½" x 2 ½".

Rail Fence Unit should measure 2 ½" x 2 ½".

Square Unit should measure 2 ½" x 2 ½".

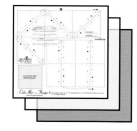

Make 8 Half Square Triangle Units from each Recipe Card.
Make 280 total.

Make 8 Rail Fence Units from each Recipe Card.
Make 280 total.

Make 2 Square Units from each Recipe Card.
Make 70 total.

Assemble Block using matching fabric.

Meringue Block One should measure 6 ½″ x 6 ½″.

Make 1 Block from each Recipe Card.

Make 35 total.

Assemble Block using matching fabric.

Meringue Block Two should measure 6 ½″ x 6 ½″.

Make 1 Block from each Recipe Card.

Make 35 total.

MERINGUE QUILT

FINISH IT UP

Assemble Quilt Center. Pay close attention to block placement. Press rows in alternating directions.
Quilt Center should measure 42 ½" x 60 ½".

Piece the Solid 4 ½" x WOF strips end to end.

Subcut into:

> 2 - 4 ½" x 60 ½" strips (Side Borders)
>
> 2 - 4 ½" x 50 ½" strips (Top and Bottom Borders)

Attach the Side Borders.

Attach the Top and Bottom Borders.

Piece the 2 ½" x WOF strips end to end for binding.

Quilt and bind as desired.

BUTTERCREAM QUILT

QUILT INGREDIENTS

One	Cake Mix Recipe #7	
	35 - Recipe Cards	Blocks
One	Print Layer Cake	
	35 - 10" squares	Blocks
One	Solid Layer Cake	
	35 - 10" squares	Blocks
2 ⅓ yards	Solid	
	60 - 2" x 6 ½" rectangles	Sashing
	13 - 2" x WOF strips	Sashing
	8 - 3 ½" x WOF strips	Border
¾ yard	Binding	
	8 - 2 ½" x WOF strips	
5 yards	Backing	

LET'S GET STARTED

With right sides facing, layer a Print 10" square with a Solid 10" square.

Follow instructions on page 3.

Large Half Square Triangle Unit should measure 3 ½" x 3 ½".

Small Half Square Triangle Unit should measure 2" x 2".

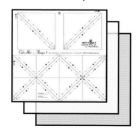

Make 4 Large Half Square Triangle Units from each Recipe Card.

Make 140 total.

Make 16 Small Half Square Triangle Units from each Recipe Card.

Make 560 total.

Assemble Unit using matching fabric.

Buttercream Unit should measure 3 ½" x 3 ½".

Make 4 Units from each Recipe Card.

Make 140 total.

Assemble Block using matching fabric. Pay close attention to unit placement.

Buttercream Block One should measure 6 ½" x 6 ½".

Make 1 Block from each Recipe Card.

Make 35 total.

Assemble Block using matching fabric. Pay close attention to unit placement.

Buttercream Block Two should measure 6 ½" x 6 ½".

Make 1 Block from each Recipe Card.

Make 35 total.

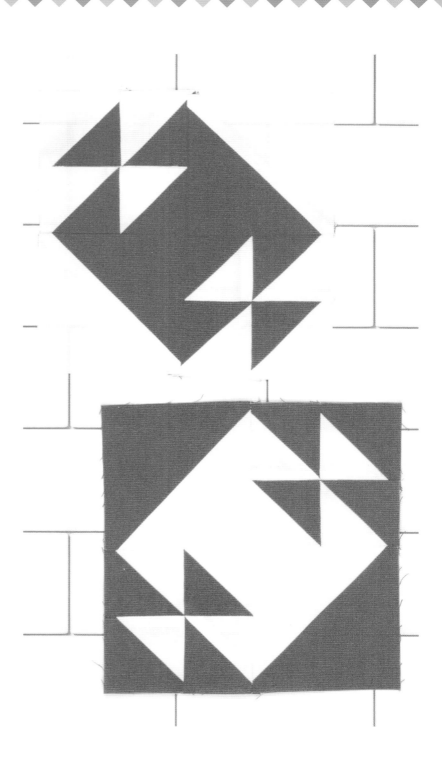

BUTTERCREAM QUILT

FINISH IT UP

Piece the Solid 2" x WOF strips end to end.

Subcut into:

> 9 - 2" x 51 ½" strips (Sashing)

Assemble Quilt Center using the Sashing. Pay close attention to block placement. Press toward the Solid.

Quilt Center should measure 51 ½" x 74".

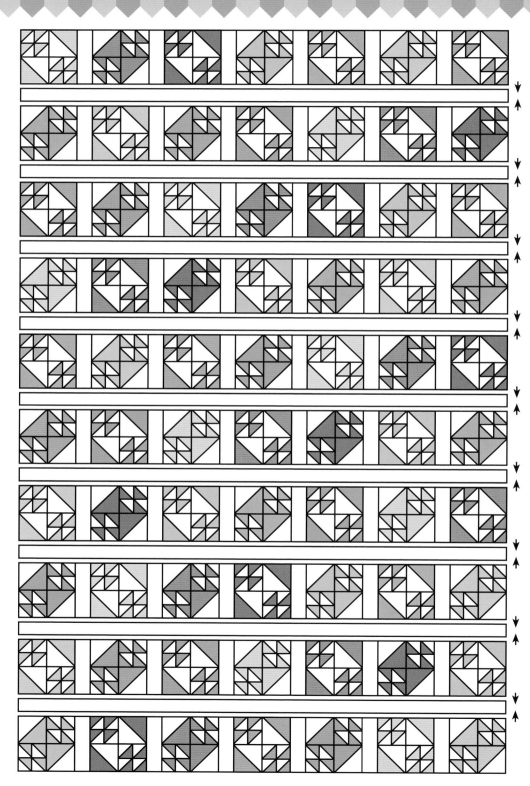

Piece the Solid 3 ½" x WOF strips end to end.

Subcut into:

    2 - 3 ½" x 74" strips (Side Borders)

    2 - 3 ½" x 57 ½" strips (Top and Bottom Borders)

Attach the Side Borders.

Attach the Top and Bottom Borders.

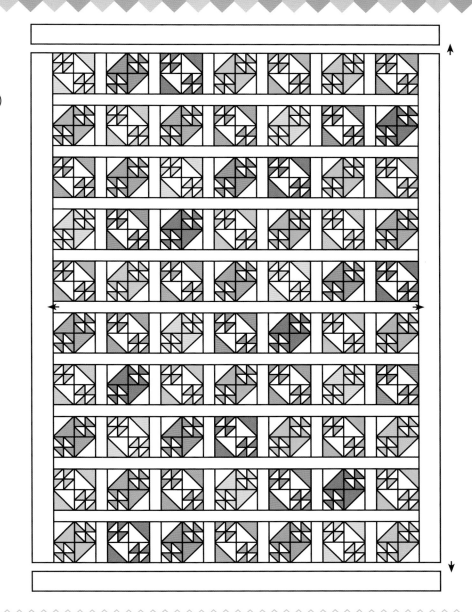

Piece the 2 ½" x WOF strips end to end for binding.

Quilt and bind as desired.

TIRAMISU QUILT

QUILT INGREDIENTS

One	Cake Mix Recipe #7	
	35 - Recipe Cards	Blocks
One	Print Moda Layer Cake	
	35 - 10" squares	Blocks
One	Solid Layer Cake	
	35 - 10" squares	Blocks
2 ¾ yards	Solid	
	140 - 2" squares	Blocks
	28 - 2" x 9 ½" rectangles	Sashing
	9 - 2" x WOF strips	Sashing
	8 - 5" x WOF strips	Border
¾ yard	Binding	
	8 - 2 ½" x WOF strips	
5 ⅛ yards	Backing	

LET'S GET STARTED

With right sides facing, layer a Print 10" square with a Solid 10" square.

Follow instructions on page 3.

Large Half Square Triangle Unit should measure 3 ½" x 3 ½".

Small Half Square Triangle Unit should measure 2" x 2".

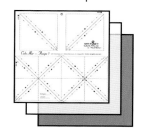

Make 4 Large Half Square Triangle Units from each Recipe Card.

Make 140 total.

Make 16 Small Half Square Triangle Units from each Recipe Card.

Make 560 total.

Assemble Unit using matching fabric.

Double Half Square Triangle Unit One should measure 2″ x 3 ½″.

Make 4 Units from each Recipe Card.

Make 140 total.

Assemble Unit using matching fabric.

Double Half Square Triangle Unit Two should measure 2″ x 3 ½″.

Make 4 Units from each Recipe Card.

Make 140 total.

Assemble Unit using matching fabric and one Solid 2″ square.

Tiramisu Unit One should measure 5″ x 5″.

Make 4 Units from 18 Recipe Cards.

Make 72 total.

Assemble Block using matching fabric.

Tiramisu Block One should measure 9 ½″ x 9 ½″.

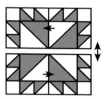

Make 1 Block from 18 Recipe Cards.

Make 18 total.

Assemble Unit using matching fabric and one Solid 2″ square.

Tiramisu Unit Two should measure 5″ x 5″.

Make 4 Units from 17 Recipe Cards.

Make 68 total.

Assemble Block using matching fabric.

Tiramisu Block Two should measure 9 ½″ x 9 ½″.

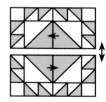

Make 1 Block from 17 Recipe Cards.

Make 17 total.

TIRAMISU QUILT

FINISH IT UP

Piece the Solid 2" x WOF strips end to end.

Subcut into:

>   6 - 2" x 51 ½" strips (Sashing)

Assemble Quilt Center using the Sashing. Pay close attention to block placement. Press toward the Solid.

Quilt Center should measure 51 ½" x 72 ½".

Piece the Solid 5" x WOF strips end to end.

Subcut into:

      2 - 5" x 72 ½" strips (Side Borders)

      2 - 5" x 60 ½" strips (Top and Bottom Borders)

Attach the Side Borders.

Attach the Top and Bottom Borders.

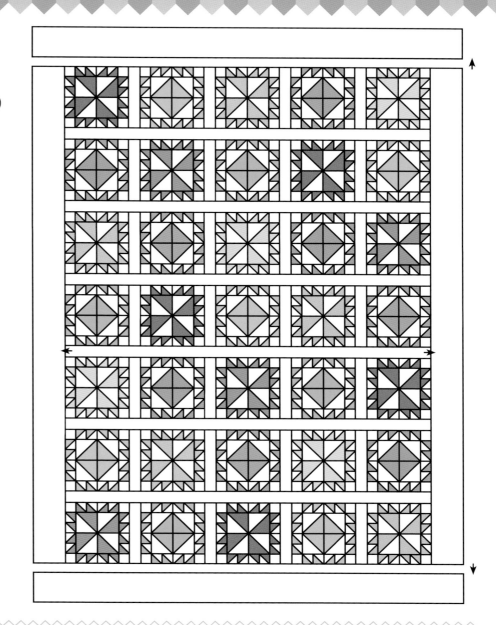

Piece the 2 ½" x WOF strips end to end for binding.

Quilt and bind as desired.

CHEESECAKE QUILT

62 ½" x 84 ½"

QUILT INGREDIENTS

One	Cake Mix Recipe #8	
	35 - Recipe Cards	Blocks
One	Print Layer Cake	
	35 - 10" squares	Blocks
One	Solid Layer Cake	
	35 - 10" squares	Blocks
3 ¼ yards	Solid	
	35 - 3 ½" squares	Blocks
	70 - 1 ½" x 2 ½" rectangles	Blocks
	70 - 1 ½" squares	Blocks
	28 - 2 ½" x 9 ½" rectangles	Sashing
	9 - 2 ½" x WOF strips	Sashing
	8 - 5" x WOF strips	Border
⅞ yard	Binding	
	9 - 2 ½" x WOF strips	
5 ¼ yards	Backing	

LET'S GET STARTED

With right sides facing, layer a Print 10" square with a Solid 10" square.

Follow instructions on page 3.

Large Half Square Triangle Unit should measure 3 ½" x 3 ½".

Small Half Square Triangle Unit should measure 1 ½" x 1 ½".

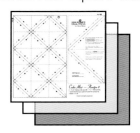

Make 4 Large Half Square Triangle Units from each Recipe Card.

Make 140 total.

Make 30 Small Half Square Triangle Units from each Recipe Card.

Make 1,050 total.

Assemble Unit using matching fabric, one
Solid 1 ½" x 2 ½" rectangle and one Solid 1 ½" square.

Cheesecake Unit One should measure 3 ½" x 3 ½".

Make 2 Units from each Recipe Card.

Make 70 total.

Assemble Unit using matching fabric.

Cheesecake Unit Two should measure 3 ½" x 3 ½".

Make 2 Units from each Recipe Card.

Make 70 total.

Assemble Block using matching fabric and one
Solid 3 ½" square.

Cheesecake Block should measure 9 ½" x 9 ½".

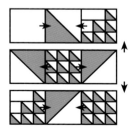   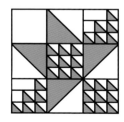

Make 1 Block from each Recipe Card.

Make 35 total.

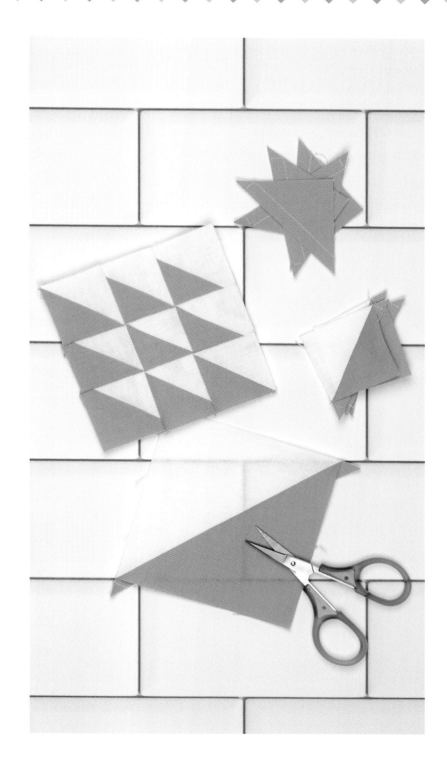

CHEESECAKE QUILT

FINISH IT UP

Piece the Solid 2 ½" x WOF strips end to end.

Subcut into:

> 6 - 2 ½" x 53 ½" strips (Sashing)

Assemble Quilt Center using the Sashing. Pay close attention to block placement. Press toward the Solid.

Quilt Center should measure 53 ½" x 75 ½".

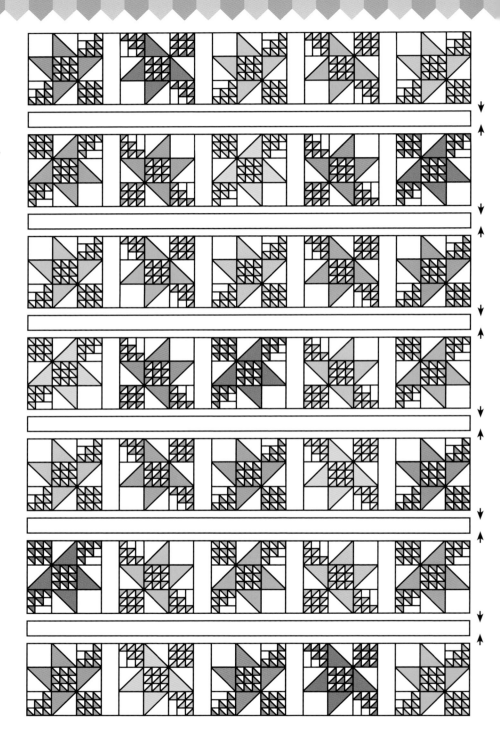

Piece the Solid 5" x WOF strips end to end.

Subcut into:

      2 - 5" x 75 ½" strips (Side Borders)

      2 - 5" x 62 ½" strips (Top and Bottom Borders)

Attach the Side Borders.

Attach the Top and Bottom Borders.

Piece the 2 ½" x WOF strips end to end for binding.

Quilt and bind as desired.

PETIT FOUR QUILT

57 ½" x 77 ½"

QUILT INGREDIENTS

One	Cake Mix Recipe #8	
	35 - Recipe Cards	Blocks
One	Print Layer Cake	
	35 - 10" squares	Blocks
One	Solid Layer Cake	
	35 - 10" squares	Blocks
2 ½ yards	Solid	
	28 - 2 ½" x 8 ½" rectangles	Sashing
	9 - 2 ½" x WOF strips	Sashing
	8 - 5" x WOF strips	Border
¾ yard	Binding	
	8 - 2 ½" x WOF strips	
4 ⅞ yards	Backing	

LET'S GET STARTED

With right sides facing, layer a Print 10" square with a Solid 10" square.

Follow instructions on page 3.

Large Half Square Triangle Unit should measure 3 ½" x 3 ½".

Small Half Square Triangle Unit should measure 1 ½" x 1 ½".

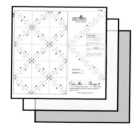

Make 4 Large Half Square Triangle Units from each Recipe Card.

Make 140 total.

Make 30 Small Half Square Triangle Units from each Recipe Card.

Make 1,050 total.

Assemble Unit using matching fabric.

Top Petit Four Unit should measure 1 ½" x 3 ½".

Make 4 Units from each Recipe Card.

Make 140 total.

Assemble Unit using matching fabric.

Left Petit Four Unit should measure 1 ½" x 3 ½".

Make 4 Units from each Recipe Card.

Make 140 total.

Assemble Unit using matching fabric.

Petit Four Unit should measure 4 ½" x 4 ½".

Make 4 Units from each Recipe Card.

Make 140 total.

YOU WILL NOT USE ALL SMALL HALF SQUARE TRIANGLE UNITS!

Assemble Block.

Petit Four Block should measure 8 ½" x 8 ½".

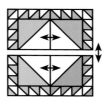

Make 35 total.

PETIT FOUR QUILT

FINISH IT UP

Piece the Solid 2 ½" x WOF strips end to end.

Subcut into:

> 6 - 2 ½" x 48 ½" strips (Sashing)

Assemble Quilt Center using the Sashing. Press toward the Solid.

Quilt Center should measure 48 ½" x 68 ½".

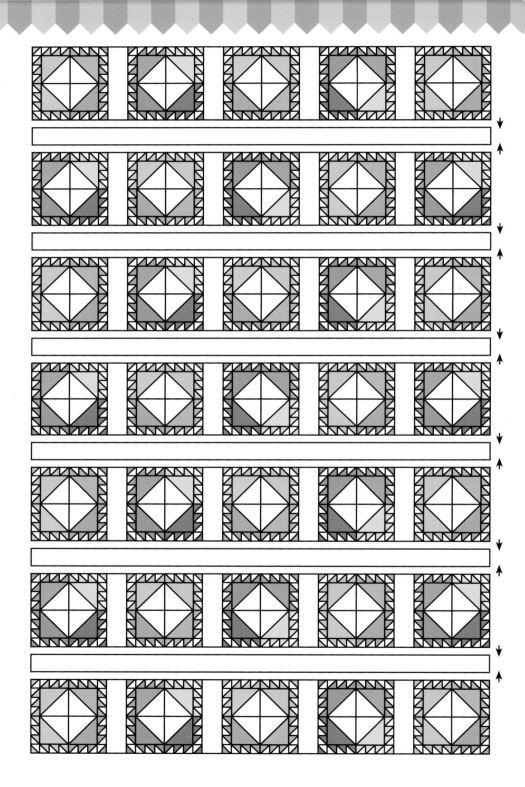